LINES

Read. Feel. Live.

Muhammad Fahad

/ BookLeaf
Publishing
India | USA | UK

Made with ❤ on the BookLeaf Publishing Platform
www.bookleafpub.in
www.bookleafpub.com

Dedication

To the Almighty, for the gift of this art,

And to my parents, who gave me my start.

For my siblings and friends, there with me each day,

For my students, who heard what I had to say.

And to the reader, who now takes this to heart,

May you find your own story playing its part.

Preface

The book you now hold is a curated collection of
verses, a tapestry woven from reflections both
recent and long-held. It is a journey into some of
life's most essential questions, and each poem is a
footstep along that path.

Within these pages, the poems contemplate the
temporary nature of our existence, reminding us
that all paths must, at last, lead back to the earth.
They look back, wondering if we can ever truly
mend the past, and turn to the soul's own court to
weigh the heavy choice between forgiving and
forgetting. These verses do not shy away from life's
Cimmerian shadows, but they consistently reach for
the light - for the resilience of hope, for the quiet
power of a poem to keep a soul alive, and for the
simple bliss found in a peaceful moment.

This collection is, in many ways, a series of
personal meditations, motivations offered to those I
care for, and questions long posed to myself. Yet,
my greatest hope is that these words might,
perhaps, resonate beyond my own story and find a
home in yours. Whether you are seeking a spark of

motivation, a moment of quiet realisation, or a reminder that friendship can feel like everything, I hope you find it here.

I leave you now to wander among these lines, where my path ends, and yours may perhaps begin.

Acknowledgements

First and foremost, I offer my deepest gratitude and reverence to the Almighty, who is the sole source of any ability I have to create. Every word is a testament to that divine grace.

To my parents, I extend my profound thanks. Your unwavering support and belief in me have been the bedrock of my life's journey.

To my siblings and friends, thank you for being constant companions. Your encouragement, wise counsel, and shared laughter have been invaluable sources of motivation and hope.

To my students, whose bright minds and curiosity are a daily inspiration, thank you. You remind me of the joy found in learning and expression.

And finally, to all who will read and perhaps find a piece of themselves in these lines: the appreciators of this work, I thank you for the great honour of your time and attention.

1. Mud Indeed!

Always and forever
Before and now
Clearly disguised
Don't know how

Everyone everything everywhere
Fallen and fooled and fumed
Growth is one's hope, Love!
Higher above the wound

Ignite the smothered
Jostle the hope
Kill the iffy
Lift the rope

My blood, your blood
Neither same nor apart
Overwhelming this vie is
Petrified! Is it the heart?

Queue towards the *AJAL*
Remaining unaware though
S won't save you, sweetheart!
Trust me! There you go.

Umbrella of kindness is lingering since you
Veracity fades, but never...
Write it. Come on! You know it.
Being xenial makes way. Clever?

Yonder places with restless feet
Zenith of every being is mud indeed.

2. Going Into The Past

Going into the past and changing something
Seems tempting.

Any detrimental incident could be shunned,

a word could be avoided

silence could be escaped

foolishness could be evaded

violence could be stopped

unnecessary non violence could be left

misunderstandings could be clarified

nonchalance could be reduced

relationships could be saved

broken hearts could be mended

emptiness could be filled

grudges could be forgotten

anger could be calmed

emotions could be relived

places could be revisited

steps could be taken

steps could be retracted

trust could be placed

faith could be altered

laughter could be suppressed

tears could be held back

sentences could be changed

consequences could be faced

insanity could be lessened

sanity could be improved

evil could be opposed

expectations could be managed

justice could be pursued

injustice could be opposed

Life could be seen

LIFE COULD BE LIVED.

3. Dear, You

This world, no doubt, is an evil parasite
That eats you from inside. And outside.
It interments alive souls into the mire of self-doubt.
It tramples you into remorse - day and night.

Heed not their frivolous tongues.
Heed not the cynic ones
Simple: You can do it.
Ride your fears. Awaken inner Huns.

One true love of life: Death
Will one day claim it forever
Death can't live without life, you see.
So, never chew cud. Never.

Refusals, setbacks, opposite of victory,
Hellish stress, and fatigue, are not mystery.
More than visible, these are intangible demons.
The requisite: Psychophysical chemistry.

"No one will help me with this." You say with belief.
Reach my hand through words of mine.
Kill the iffy. Shun the weak behind.
Look, how resplendent is your resurgent shine.

4. Not Only Looking At The Surface

Observing? Yes.
Putting efforts? Yes.
Being empathetic? Yes.
Not only looking at the surface? Yes.

Yes,
These things make things better.
These things keep you aware.
These things are precious.
These things are key to peace in the long run.
These things develop faith.
These things build trust.
These things make you consistent.
These things let you think smoother.
These things clean your mind.
These things tell fewer lies.
These things escape you from drowning in vain.
These things emancipate you from immaturity.
These things refrain you from wrong decisions.

These things bring more understanding.
These things cook delicious relationships.
These things dust off the insecurities.

These things combine two alikes together.

These things cool the burning melancholy.

These things turn hate into not hate.

These things open the gates of cooperation.

These things sow the seeds of affection.

These things lay the foundation of solid bond.

These things wrap you around benevolence.

These things lead more to success.

These things wipe out the dirt of negativity.

These things rub off the pain of unnecessary ponder.

These things shoot the best 'kindness arrows'.

These things kill the iffy.

These things behold the positivity.

These things ameliorate pure emotions.

These things really do what they are supposed to,

if done with pure intention and right strength.

5. The Bliss!

Soothing scenery, peace.
No unnecessary chaos.
No commotion.
No fake realities.

Free days and free night.
Seconds to count endlessly.
No hate. No hypocrisy. No limits.
No anchors to make you tight.

A bright new day,
Where you can watch the sky.
Count the birds, then watch
them going away.

You can be quiet and think.
Quiet and think nothing at all.
Sleep. Stay awake. Read. Write.
Breathe. Smile. Blink.

Be whatever you miss
Whatever that's not evil.
No melancholy or malevolence.
Ah! The bliss.

6. Realise it, too.

You know you're alive.
Realise it, too.
You know you have food.
Realise it, too.

You know you'll die.
Realise it, too.
You know you can starve
Realise it, too.

We know everything
We see everything
We may feel everything
And we don't care, that's true

That's true
And you know it.
Realise it, too.

7. My Words For You

Hey! You have me.
Right now, my words,
If you let them be

They have it all. But they are 'Most people'
You aren't alike, you are special
Above all clichés, above all sheeple
Reminiscent of warmth in face of glacial.

He left you alone, yet left you never.
He knows. He cares. He bestows.
He lets you decide and makes you clever.
He holds. He nurtures. He grows.

Caress my words, should there be a need
Tis for you, these words
Void is volatile. Melancholy, too, indeed.
Might link you -- to the herds.

Partial goodness is no goodness.
Thy kismet aims transcendent denouement
Zap rumination. Better things on the way.
You will be rewarded. You will be reborn.

8. Precious

You are a gift from God
You are beloved
You are a stirring squad
You are above it

You can. You know it
You focus. You show it
You tackle. You sow it
You pluck. You grow it

You're what? You falter.
Your powers. You flout.
Now shun it, Precious -
This all in one doubt

No one knows
what resides in you
Only you have it in,
And it is so true

The power, the courage
The will, the brain
In all of your stories
You are the main

Remain at ease
Tis patience you need
You will savour
The success, indeed!

9. Detrimental

I behest you to
abate yourself, change your disposition.
Be flop ever now and just tumble.
Let your power go in vain.

I know that you know.
And you know that I know.
So, if I know that you know.
And that you know what I know.
Then why should we waste our time
In what we already know.

What I know is not mine
but your end.
What you know is not yours
but my victory.

Though you queer me,
I will always fight back.
Whenever you will put the light off,
I will always put it on.
There is an end of every darkness.
This is what we already know.

It's not night
which is darkness,
It's not morning
which is light.
It's the unkind
who want them to stop
but it's the kind
who stops unkind,
and never let himself stop.

Whatever you do,
do with kindness
because no darkness and no unkind
is going to be detrimental.

10. 26

Awesome is you, who inspire the pathetics.

Brave is you, who endure bad Situations.

Conspicuous is you, who unveil the positives.

Dapper is you, who absterge the vile.

Emphatic is you, who enunciate the frauds.

Fictitious is you, who actualize the humanity.

Gleaming is you, who enlighten the virtuous.

Honest is you, who do not even hope for it.

Impeccable is you, who avenge the arsonists.

Joyous is you, who enhance it in the grave.

Key is you, who unlock the door of success.

Loving is you, who hate malevolent.

Mammoth is you, who belittle the sin.

New is you, who restore true old values.

Opulent is you, who bequeath to needy.

Perennial is you, who terminate the phony.

Quintessential is you, who hold the queasy.

Robust is you, who halt the rogue.

Spearhead is you, who aggrandise the birth giver.

Tall is you, who trounce the selfish.

Unassailable is you, who assail the false.

Vivacious is you, who embrace all.

Winning is you, who lose for right.

Xantho is you, who drench in gold.

Yule is you, who sing the hymn of heart.

Zappy is you, who remain what you are.

11. Hope You Live Alive.

Smile away the tears
when you feel the wet

Cry away the pain
when you feel the burden

Sing away it cruel
when you've been reticent

Dance away it loud
when you've been handicapped

Say it hello
Tell us good bye
Hope you see bright
Hope you drink blessings
Hope you eat moon
Hope you Live Alive.

12. A Letter In Subway

She sits. She sighs.
She thinks. She tries.
She begins. She pauses.
She opens and closes

a letter in subway.

In between, she is frozen.
Being tired. Being broken.
Evading her losses.
She opens and closes

a letter in subway.

Physical and mental
Her breaths, they tremble
Yet, being flawless.
She opens and closes

a letter in subway.

Ineffable headache
Pain, she couldn't take
Though knowing the causes
She opens and closes

a letter in subway.

Slowly, it fades
And she escapes.
Pains do not feed.
When she does read -

The letter in subway.

13. Poem it is

When you bite your tongue
When you stop to try
When you lose your fun
When you start to cry

Poem it is
Which makes you feel
Poem it is
Which keeps you alive

14. The Thing Called "Hope"

With still me inside,
I lost my path's true thread,
I'm iffy and ambivalent,
precluded by my head.

The requisite skill was in me
to have it all, almost,
But I'd shy away and call it a jest,
when I should mean it the most.

Requisite techniques were with me,
but I could not apply,
My heart was lost in "what ifs,"
beneath a questioning sky.

Time and me, we both betrayed -
a sinister, silent tongue,
While I stood in a dilemma,
feeling speechless and dumb.

Some blamed me for it all,
and some blame the time,
But I looked at them together
and blamed both for the crime.

Now, I will not let me stop
until I reach the very top,
I'll be martial and kill the iffy,
and make the doubting drop.

They will see me then and say,
"That's the he in me!"
As again and again I try,
and never cease to be.

I will never, ever give up
on that slope,
And never, ever lose
the thing called "Hope."

15. I'm Not Wise

How are you?
Harmless.

What do you do?
I try.

What are you doing in your life?
Not giving up.

What do you like the most?
To help.

What do you hate the most?
Nothing.

What do you dislike?
Injustice.

What do you want the most?
Patience.

Which is your favourite language?
Silence.

What do you expect from people?
No, not from people.

What do you possess?
Good intentions.

What will you leave behind, then?
Good deeds.

What is your strength?
I understand.

What is your weakness?
I understand.

What have you achieved?
Trust.

Is that so?
I believe.

Are you sure?
Maybe naive.

What have you lost?
Hypocrisy.

Would you kill?
Already did.

What! Whom?
Negativity.

Thank God!
Every second.

What do you mean?
Gratitude.

Oh! I see.
I hope you could.

Wait! Why?
You already know.

Do I?
...

Do I?
...

Do I? You're right. I do.
You do.

You sound so wise.
However, I'm not.

Fine, I'll go.
Good luck.

For what?
To fight yourself.

And find you again?
No! To find yourself.

16. How's Life?

Life? Life is like life:
stable-unstable,
fast-slow,
peaceful-chaotic,
clear-unclear,
kind-unkind,
beautiful-ugly,
found-lost,
sane-insane,
deep-shallow,
fair-unfair,
just-unjust,
comfortable-uncomfortable,
bright-dull,
loud-quiet,
frank-austere,
smooth-rough,
gentle-hard,
forgiving-unforgiving,
black-white,
horrific-pleasant,
high-low,
in-out,
here-there,

near-far,
healing-damaging,
breathable-unbreathable,
warm-cold,
new-old,
true-false,
harmonious-troubled,
giving-taking,
blissful-grievous,
and much more.

17. Forgiving or Forgetting?

What is harder, Forgiving or Forgetting?
If a person is stronger than both,
I think neither.
What if a person is stronger than neither?
In that case, the one that requires
learning and effort
will be harder,
and will hurt.

For a person good at forgetting,
Forgetting it is, for sure.
For a person good at forgiving,
Forgiving is the cure.

For a person good at neither,
nature plays the role
Forgetting: An easier choice for brain
Forgiving? Not at all!

What happens when you forget?
You remain calm
until the memories harm.
Then, the same pain,
same trauma,

same sadness,
same melancholy
holds your head,
holds your charm,
gives you a qualm.

What happens when you forgive?
Forgive to let go(forget)?
Or
Forgive to embrace(accept the veracity)?

When you forgive and let it go,
it doesn't haunt you anymore.
Even if it does come back,
It's trivial, you already know.

On the other hand,
when you forgive and accept the facts as they are,
you become resilient and adapt and befriend the scar.
You begin living with the fact.
Hence, no chance that it does distract.

Eventually, you overcome the pain.
Above it you rise.
This makes you stronger and stronger.
Closer to wise.

18. If Only I Could Be...

If only I could be
what this world wants me to be,
I could never then be killed,
for they already would've killed me.

Nah. I'm not bothered,
not one to ponder over
what I can't lose.
It's already lost.
I lost the fear the moment I could fly.

Those freaky and evil minds
tell me to abate the good I do.
Yes! I do it anyway.
Are they so scared of what is true?

Now come on! Be what you are and let their pain
increase.
Let your wrath behead them.
Kill the myrmidon in you that's killing you.
Unveil your good and the wicked behind the lectern.
Bestow the vow of your dedication and hope;
don't get het up by the cheap greed for a selfish man's
bread.

Move!
Walk!
Prove!
Show!
Achieve.

But listen... you're right.
Yes, I was wrong.
This quest isn't possible.
And you know why?

Because you who listen are deaf.
Because you who read are dumb.
Because you who watch are blind.
And because you could act, but never did,
you are cowards.

For all of my words,
for all of my rhymes,
for all of my shouts,
despite how it hurts...

It's still gonna be the same
if words don't turn to action.
It's still gonna be the same
if we all live in false satisfaction.

So, again I say:
If only I could be
what this world wants me to be,
I could never then be killed,
for they already would've killed me.

19. Friendship = Everything

I do, you do, we do, they do have friends.
Count not on fingers; count on no hands.
It's the heart where they live, like heartbeats.
You live with them; you die without heartbeats.
You panic, it runs; it runs in your joy.
So do your friends, whether girl or boy.

It's true they laugh at you the most,
And it's true they laugh with you the most.
It's best, I say, when they talk;
They talk when we are in trouble.
It's best, I say, when they walk;
They walk to decrease our trouble.

I do, you do, we do, they do have friends.
Count not on fingers; count on no hands.
It's a pen where they live, like its ink.
You move with it; you're trash without the ink.

It's true they treat you the worst,
But it's true that they are the best.
You write your love, your secrets—all is written,
All with one, and sometimes by one it's written.

It's best, I say, when they bestow.
They bestow when we are in need.
Though an old truth, a verity it is still:
Such are the friends, indeed.

I do, you do, we do, they do have friends.
Count not on fingers; count on no hands.
It's a book where they live like words.
You are precious with them;
You are thrown out without the words.

20. Cimmerian

Drowned in Cimmerian was the whole of me,
All in this dread, and not what I could see.
Seeing with my eyes was all in vain;
Vanity! Veracity! Yes! I am in pain.

I never did muse to see that light's flow,
And never want to lose that shine below.
The moment I try, I drown in again;
For me, it's not a play to shun that pain.

Just like a curse, it is embraced so tight,
My enemy is sleep and the funeral night.
The task was all to pass that endless time,
To make it right and get back that shine.

A lament for a capricious mind,
Leaving all my sanity behind.
Incessantly, I heard the clamour,
Exerted my all, but still held by its glamour.

It was not what it used to be,
Like desperate water poured into the sea.
This is the sea I drown in the most,
To get back to the life I want to host.

Do no harm, and do no hurt to anyone.
Something everyone tries with everyone.
Give love, and take love from everyone.

Yes, I need, and yes, I want.
To be deprived - please tell me don't.
I'll make it fine, all of it for you;
Forever, it's you in me, and I in you.

21. Before I Die

Before I die,
Let me not surrender.
Let me be myself.
Let me be tender.

Let me be defender.
Let me be mender.
Let me be patient.
Let me be lender.

Let me be laughter.
Let me be drafter.
Let me be peace.
Let me be crafter.

Let me be fun.
Let me not run
From stars and moon.
And from the sun.

Let me be available.
Let me not fear
The evil or failure.
Is that clear?

Let me decide
What I want.
For what I need,
Is here, indeed.

Let me love.
Let me care.
Let me hold.
Let me spare.

Let me look.
Let me cook.
Let me write
My own book.

Let me help.
Let me forgive.
Let me thank.
Let me relive.

Let me not spoil
Any relation.
Let me experience
Every nation.

Let me be free

Let me try.
When I escape,
Please don't cry.

The words aren't enough.
The list isn't over.
The wishes of men.
Of drunk or sober.

There's no limit
To what I want.
Maybe I get'em.
Maybe I don't.

No matter what,
Let me be calm.
Let me be calm,
Whether winning or not.

Let me be alive,
Before I die.
Before I die,
Let me survive.

www.ingramcontent.com/pod-product-compliance
Lightning Source LLC
Chambersburg PA
CBHW070501050426
42449CB00012B/3077